Church Banner Designs

72 Unique Ideas
Using Calico, Batik, and Other Cotton Prints

By Joyce Bowers

D1088967

CONCORDIA PUBLISHING HOUSE • SAINT LOUIS

Dedicated to Pastor Peter A. Hellstedt and the
people of Grace Lutheran Church, Mount Prospect, Illinois,
who have encouraged and supported their banner lady.

Copyright © 2007 Concordia Publishing House
3558 S. Jefferson Avenue
St. Louis, MO 63118-3968
1-800-325-3040 • www.cph.org

Written by Joyce Bowers • Illustrated by Joyce Bowers

Manufactured in the United States of America

1 2 3 4 5 6 7 8 9 10   16 15 14 13 12 11 10 09 08 07

Contents

Introduction

Welcome to a new world of banner making! Are you a beginner, intrigued with the possibility of banner making? Are you an experienced crafter looking for new ideas? Either way, this book is for you. I am delighted to share with you what I have learned and developed over the course of three decades of my own banner making.

When I began making them thirty years ago, banners were typically constructed with burlap backgrounds and felt designs and letters. The result was often informal, bordering on crude. Over the years, banner making has evolved to favor more refined styles, some of which require considerable design and sewing skills and demand a significant amount of time.

To encourage you in your own banner making, most of the patterns in this book are relatively simple. The construction techniques are also simple and straightforward, requiring no special skills beyond the familiar know-how of "crafty ladies" who are members of any congregation. And the time involved in making them can be as little or as much as you choose.

I have found that the key to making beautiful, eye-catching banners using the patterns and methods in this book is choosing colors and fabrics. Although in a black-and-white book it is impossible to convey the impact of artful combinations of fabrics, braids, and borders, my hope is that the descriptions and designs I offer here are enough to help you get started.

My goal is that as you read this book and think about how these designs might be displayed in your church, you are inspired to create banners that motivate and inspire … to the glory of God.

Joyce Bowers

Banner Basics

Using Calico for Banners

As my banner making has developed, I have used more and more calico—lightweight cotton fabrics that are designed for quilting. Happily, quilting has enjoyed a renaissance in recent years, and hundreds of calicos are readily available. Floral prints and other patterns, used judiciously, can make striking, effective banners. Subtle tie-dye and batik prints also make wonderful backgrounds and lend elegance to simple designs.

Computers and Photocopiers

Advances in technology have greatly enhanced banner making. Computer word processing and design programs provide a wide variety of fonts or letter styles and can print letters four or more inches tall, which allows styles of lettering to complement the banner designs and give the finished banners a professional appearance. Photocopiers have also become more sophisticated in recent years, making it easier than ever to enlarge patterns accurately instead of spending hours doing it by hand.

The Church Year

This book is organized around the Church Year as observed by Lutherans, Episcopalians, Roman Catholics, and other Christian church bodies. The year begins with Advent, four Sundays prior to Christmas, and ends with Christ the King Sunday in late November. Each season has traditional colors and themes that are reflected in the banner patterns in this book.

The longest season is the Time of the Church, which includes the Sundays between Pentecost and Advent. For that season, I offer banner designs that have themes and colors not included in the seasons of Advent, Christmas, Epiphany, Lent, Easter, and Pentecost. These designs are in the last three sections of the book: non-seasonal, Christian symbols, and church boards.

Choosing Symbols and Images

When I choose symbols or images for banners, I look for those that are aesthetically pleasing, simple enough to reproduce in fabric without looking cluttered, and familiar enough to convey meaning to the typical church member. I often use traditional Christian symbols that visually reinforce our heritage of faith.

Choosing Words

When words are used in combination with an image, I choose a short phrase. If words constitute the main design of the banner, a longer phrase may be used. Words may be taken from Bible verses, hymns, or the liturgy (see page 95). Often they are commonly used phrases or basic concepts of the season.

As with symbols or images, words should be aesthetically pleasing and simple. At the same time they should inspire and educate the average worshiper. When I get stuck and can't decide what words to use for a particular banner, I consult my pastor. He gives me suggestions that reflect his expertise in the Bible, theology, and effective communication.

Choosing Colors

Most of the patterns in this book are for seasons of the Church Year and use traditional liturgical colors (such as purple for Lent) for the background. Depending on where the banner hangs, I may add other colors as part of the image. When I make banners for the walls on the sides of the sanctuary, I use more striking color combinations. Banners that hang near the altar have simpler designs and color combinations and are coordinated with the paraments (hangings on the altar, pulpit, and lectern).

Fabrics for Backgrounds

The key to making beautiful banners is the choice of fabrics. Once I've identified the banner design, the background fabric is usually the first thing I choose. If the background is a solid color, I look for a fabric that is heavier than calico, often with a design in the weave, a satiny sheen, or another attractive quality. If the background is a calico print or batik, I look for subtle, monochromatic prints with different shades of the same color or similar colors. Prints that look like marble and tie-dyes with subtle shadings are excellent.

If the background is a major part of the design of the banner, a print with two colors may be effective, perhaps with gold or silver highlights. Generally I avoid large floral or geometric designs, and I also avoid highly contrasting colors. If the image is very simple, the background can be a bit more striking.

When shopping for combinations of fabrics, I always drape them side-by-side in the fabric store and then move as far away as I can to see how they look from a distance. I often find that a combination that looks great up close is not quite right viewed from a distance.

When choosing the background fabric, be sure to keep in mind the ease of working with it. Calicos and other cotton or cotton blend woven fabrics are excellent. A gorgeous soft or stretchy fabric may be tempting, but if it is hard to manage, you will regret giving in to the temptation, as your finished banner will have crooked edges, wrinkles where the design is attached, or other undesirable results. Background fabric needs to have good body so it stays put and doesn't slide around when you are working with it. Background fabric also needs to be quite smooth, although it can have some texture such as a linen-like weave or brocade. Some people use felt for banners because it doesn't need to be hemmed, but I find it too thick, stretchy, and fuzzy for my style of banner making.

Fabrics to avoid include soft, drapey fabrics such as crepes and most rayons. Avoid stretchy fabrics such as knits, no matter how beautiful they are! Also stay away from synthetics with a low tolerance for heat. Check the fabric information on the end of the bolt; if it says to press with a warm iron, you don't want it. Finally, designs I've included here are not suitable for a fabric with nap, such as corduroy or velour.

When I construct the banner background, I sew a ¾-inch hem on each side, and a 3-inch casing at the top and bottom to hold the rods. I do not line banners, as it is unnecessary, adds extra work, and makes banners heavier and more bulky.

Enlarging Patterns

Designs in this book can be enlarged using a photocopier. High-quality copiers may be found in libraries, business supply stores, and copy centers. To enlarge the design to full size, the pattern has to be enlarged in sections. First, enlarge it to the largest size that will fit on the paper available, usually 11 x 17 inches. Then, to bring it to its full size, fold the 11 x 17-inch copy and enlarge it section by section. When enlarging sections, be sure to refold the original for each exposure so there is overlap in the enlarged sections (this makes it easier to assemble), and then tape the full-size sections together. It helps to pencil an X in several places in the overlap area to make it easier to assemble the sections accurately. (See illustration above.)

With a little math and a handheld calculator, I obtain the exact final size by calculating the percentage of enlargement needed. For example, if a finished design needs to be 23 inches wide and after two or three enlargements you now have 16 inches, divide 23 by 16 to obtain the percent of enlargement needed: $23 \div 16 = 1.4375$ or 144 percent. Most up-to-date copy machines allow you to enter the exact percentage of enlargement desired.

Proportion of Design to Banner Size

Most of my banners are 54 inches long and 36

inches wide. In my experience, the best proportion seems to be a design about 24 inches wide, leaving six inches on each side. If a minor part of the design is wider than the rest, it can be closer to the edge, but I always leave at least 4 inches on the sides. A good rule of thumb is to have the words and images about two-thirds to three-fourths the width of the banner. When I use borders, they are generally about 4 inches from the top and bottom edge.

A few banner patterns in this book are designed with borders to give you an idea of the proportion I use; see pages 86–94. Your banners may be a different size or shape than mine, so most of the pages in this book show only the central design and words.

Attaching Designs and Decorations

My two standbys for attaching fabrics and trims are fusible interfacing for bonding fabrics to backgrounds and craft glue for braids, fringe, or lettering cut from vinyl upholstery. Both of these products are available at fabric and craft stores.

There are many types of glue for fabrics and crafts. My favorite is craft glue because it is thick and tacky, and also because it dries slowly enough to allow some adjustments while the glue is still moist. It dries clear, so extra little bits of glue hardly show.

I recommend that you experiment with the variety of bonding agents that are currently available in your local stores. I favor a brand of fusible interfacing that is of heavier weight and has a lower bonding temperature, but you may find a different kind of product that works best for you. Be sure to experiment with both heavier and lighter weight fusible interfacing. I've found that heavier weight works best for permanently bonding fabric, but it cannot be used for appliqué because it quickly gums up needles. Lighter weight interfacing is useful for holding an appliqué in place but does not create a strong bond when attaching pieces of fabric to the background.

Outlining Designs and Words

I outline most of the designs and words on my banners, as outlining adds great depth and beauty. I most often use fabric paint that comes in squeeze bottles and is sold in fabric and craft stores. Unfortunately, getting a smooth line with a consistent width is not easy! It is important to shake the paint down into the tip frequently because air bubbles will pop when they are squeezed out, making small mess-

es. If you are not accustomed to working with these paints, it is best to practice on scrap fabric before applying paint to the banner.

No matter how carefully I apply it, I am often disappointed with the way the paint looks. The next step is to take a round toothpick and drag it through the line before the paint sets. It is amazing how much this smoothes out the line of paint! Also, I find that by the time the paint dries and I hang the banner, the little imperfections are not noticeable.

Another option for outlining is trim or braid. I often use narrow braid for simple designs, and in fact braid may make a major contribution to the overall banner. When buying braid for outlining, be sure to test it to see how easily it will go around curves or corners. I use craft glue to apply braid.

Lettering is usually too complicated to outline with braid. Sometimes I cut letters from vinyl upholstery, which makes the lettering stand out without having to outline it. I can cut smooth edges with sharp scissors, and the thickness adds a three-dimensional effect to the banner. Vinyl with smooth knit backing is easier to work with than vinyl with fuzzy backing, since the design is traced on the back of the fabric. Vinyl letters must be glued to the banner. Of course the range of colors is much more limited with vinyl.

Quilting stores also sell very narrow (⅛") iron-on bias tape in a few colors. I have not used it for banners, but you may wish to experiment with it. A miniature iron attached to a straight handle is used to iron it in place.

Borders

Many of the banners I create have borders at the top and bottom. A few have borders on all four sides, using rounded corners if the border is braid and mitered corners if it is ribbon. Borders are typically applied about 3 or 4 inches from the edge. I use a variety of materials; see page 86 for some examples.

BRAID OR FRINGE. I usually use braid or fringe at least 2 inches wide. The cut ends ravel easily, so they need to be sealed; I use a fray sealer, available in fabric and craft stores. It is a clear, runny liquid that comes in a small squeeze bottle with a narrow applicator top. A drop or two soaks into the fibers and seals them as it dries, and is nearly invisible when dry.

Occasionally I use a woven type of braid if it has colors that coordinate with the banner. I apply the braid by sewing or gluing it, then I wrap the ends of around to the back of the banner and sew or glue them in place.

LACE. I usually choose Cluny lace, which is heavier and more visible from a distance. Lace may be stitched on or applied with glue. I rarely use fine-textured lace, but I did use some with gold highlights on the Christmas banners shown on pages 21 and 22. A narrow gold braid outlining the angels makes a nice finishing touch.

FABRIC. If I use fabric for a border, I look for one with a design in a stripe or squares. See page 86 for examples. A fabric border can be very effective if the colors match those in the main image. I might put grosgrain ribbon on each side of the border if the stripe design is too narrow or to highlight a color. Fabric or wide ribbon borders are applied with fusible interfacing as described on page 8; narrow ribbon is usually glued on.

RIBBON. Wide grosgrain ribbon may be used for borders or for a frame on all sides of the banner. When using ribbon, check to see if it shrinks when ironed. If it does, iron it with a hot iron before use to preshrink it.

Hanging Banners

Most of my banners are 36 x 54 inches, and I use plain unfinished ½-inch wooden dowels in the top and bottom. I cut the top dowel about ½-inch longer than the banner is wide to facilitate hanging, and the bottom dowel is cut slightly shorter than the banner width so it doesn't show. The weight of the bottom dowel helps the banner hang straight, and carrying banners from one place to another is much easier when you can grasp both dowels together in one hand.

Home improvement and hardware stores sell 48-inch dowels that are cheaper than the 36-inch dowels sold at craft stores. I usually roll a few on the floor before purchasing them to find the ones that are straight, as many are slightly warped.

To hang the banner on a single nail, hook, or banner stand, you need to add a cord. I put thumbtacks partway into the ends of the top dowel, tie heavy cotton string around the tacks, and then pound the tacks in the rest of the way with a hammer, holding the string securely. The loose ends of the string are trimmed to about 4 inches and taped to the dowel with masking tape so they are hidden inside the cas-

ing of the banner. You can attach the string to one end before you insert the dowel into the banner casing; the other end has to be done with the dowel in the casing.

Decorative curtain rods with finials make much more elegant hangers for banners, but my philosophy is that the banner is the focus of attention, not the rod. If you are making a lot of banners, cost may be a major factor. Also, curtain rods with decorative finials can be bulky to store.

Making Your Own Banner Designs

I hope this book inspires you to use similar techniques with designs from other sources. This is the fun part for me.

IMAGES. I'm always on the lookout for banner possibilities, and I have an idea box overflowing with greeting cards, clip art, logos from stationery, illustrations from publications, brochures, and Christian catalogs—anything that might inspire a banner design. To be respectful of copyrights and creative property, I do not use a design exactly as is. I enlarge the idea with a photocopier until it fits on an 8½ x 11-inch sheet of paper, then I modify and adapt it using pencil and tracing paper. If the design is simple and symmetrical, I use ¼-inch graph paper. Then I enlarge my pencil design to full size, using a photocopier as described on page 7.

With a computerized design program, the process is similar but it is done electronically. I scan the idea, import it into one layer and lock the layer. Then I create the adaptation in a second and maybe third layer if it has several components. I then hide the first layer, lock the image layers, and add words in a final layer. It sounds simple, but is tricky until you are familiar with a design program.

WORDS. Many of the banners I make have words in addition to images. I often use the fonts in word processing programs. If you have a word processing or design program with multiple fonts and the capacity to print them in any size, you are in business!

When I am planning a banner with a finished size of 36 x 54 inches, I make a 1:6 scale drawing of 6 x 9 inches (1 inch on the pattern equals 6 inches on the finished banner). I draw a box of that size on standard paper and experiment with what font size looks best in it.

Type size is measured in points; the default size for letters is usually 12-point type. Typically, the type size on my scale drawing is between 75 points and 100 points. For the actual letter patterns, I print the letters at six times the point size, so a 75-point letter on the scale design is printed out with 450-point letters for the actual pattern. Only a few letters fit on a page at that size, but the result is clear, ready-to-use patterns.

Often the letters are too light in weight (the lines are too narrow) for use on a banner even if they are enlarged to the height and width desired. When this happens, try printing them in bold. If that doesn't do the trick, you can cut the letter patterns slightly outside the printed area. If still more weight is needed, after you trace the letter onto fabric backed by fusible interfacing, you can cut the finished letters another smidgen outside the tracing.

I often make adjustments in the letters because they don't look right to me once they are enlarged. I may reduce the size of a flourish, round off square corners, or shorten or lengthen part of a letter to improve the final design.

I wish you great pleasure and satisfaction in your banner making, whether you use my patterns, design your own, or do a combination. You may wish to consult other banner books for ideas or other creative variations. Whatever you do, I hope you enjoy your effort and, more so, that it serves your church and our God.

A Spirituality of Banner Making

Making banners is one of my favorite activities. I love the colors, the fabrics, the creative expression, the problems that arise and challenge me, and the satisfaction of solving them. But banner making has meaning for me that is far deeper than a pleasant, creative hobby. It is a vital element of my spiritual life. No other activity has given me such satisfaction in expressing the gifts and calling God has given. Here are some of the reasons.

CREATING BEAUTY: God, our Creator, takes pleasure in creating beauty. After completing the creation on the sixth day, "God saw everything that He had made, and behold, it was very good" (Genesis 1:31). When we make something beautiful, we reflect God's creative nature, just as when we show love to others, we reflect God's loving nature.

BEAUTIFYING GOD'S HOUSE: When I read about the first house of God—the tabernacle or huge tent described in Exodus—I identify with the people who helped build it. Ordinary people donated their treas-ured possessions of gold jewelry, yarn, and fine linen for the use of artisans. "Every skillful woman spun with her hands, and they all brought what they had spun in blue and purple and scarlet yarns and fine twined linen. All the women *whose hearts stirred them to use their skill* spun the goats' hair" (Exodus 35:25–26). "All the men and women . . . *whose heart moved them* to bring anything for the work . . . brought it as a freewill offering to the LORD" (Exodus 35:29).

Today, it is rare for us to participate personally in the creation of beauty for the house of God, but when our hearts move us to use our skill in designing and making banners that will hang in the sanctuary, we follow those blessed women. God is honored whenever we use our talents for good purposes; it is especially meaningful to beautify a house of worship. For me, banner making is a joyful privilege.

ENHANCING WORSHIP: When I enter a sanctuary with majestic stained-glass windows, my spirit is lifted and I eagerly anticipate what will happen in that beautiful place. Banners, along with lighting, flowers, candles, and paraments, help create a sense of inspiration and motivation even in modest sanctuaries. My attention is drawn to the banners before the service begins, helping me prepare my heart and mind for worship.

STRENGTHENING IDENTITY: I intentionally use familiar, traditional symbols and words in my banners. I strive to remind my congregation (and myself) that we are part of a legacy of faith that goes back thousands of years. Symbols such as a Celtic cross or the alpha and omega help remind me that I am part of a great company of saints. Symbols enrich the ancient, traditional words of prayers and creeds, and in an era of overwhelming change, traditions help anchor and root us in our identity as God's beloved children.

GUIDED BY THE SPIRIT: One of the most creative aspects of making banners is choosing fabrics, braids, and borders. This often time-consuming process can be a meditative experience. As I browse in fabric stores, I ponder the meaning of the symbol or words of a particular banner design and how best to convey that meaning to worshipers. Sometimes I am blessed with an awareness of the Spirit's guidance in choosing specific fabrics or working out the details of expressing a concept in fabric art. The sense of God's presence and influence in the creative process gives me deep, quiet, enduring joy.

THE GIFT OF COLOR: I believe that color is one of God's greatest creations. Many years ago, my husband and I served as missionaries in West Africa. One December, we flew from Monrovia, Liberia, to Frankfurt, Germany, en route to the United States. We left tropical Africa with its emerald rice fields and riots of flowers, crystal blue skies and spectacular sunsets, and people with rich dark skin tones and extravagantly colorful clothing. We arrived in Frankfurt, where the skies were leaden, the trees were bare, and pale-faced people clad in black and dark navy walked on gray sidewalks amid gray buildings. My spirit sank. It made me want to get on the next plane back to the tropics! A few years ago, while working on a large banner project for a national church gathering, I used dozens of beautiful fabrics in a wide array of colors. I became aware of how much pleasure God's gift of color gives me.

The Bottom Line

My prayer is that this book and the banner making it inspires will be a stepping stone to deeper spirituality for you. May you experience the fellowship and joy of the Holy Spirit as you invest your time and talents for God's glory.

Advent

The church year begins with Advent, a time of anticipation and longing for the Christ Child to come to us anew. In our busy lives, Advent competes for our attention with Christmas shopping, long "to do" lists, and holiday entertainment and travel. It's easy to forget what Advent is all about outside of Sunday and midweek worship. But our busy-ness and stress can also be an invitation to heartfelt prayer to the One who comes to transform us and our world. The themes of these banners invite us to just such prayer and reflection, whether in snatches of time while on the run or during longer times of quiet meditation.

The traditional color for Advent is blue, although purple may also be used. I take the liberty of using shades of blue, teal, and turquoise.

Fling Wide the Gates! and **The King of Glory Comes!** are a pair of banners expressing joyful anticipation of the Lord's arrival. For the backgrounds, I used a medium blue calico with a subtle design enhanced by a gold pattern. I used somewhat muted colors in the stained-glass window above the open doors because it is not the focal point. The Chi-Rho in **The King of Glory Comes!** is often used to represent Christ as King. It is dark blue and surrounded with gold flashes.

Prepare the Way of the Lord was the cry of the prophets, including John the Baptist. In this banner, the Way is symbolized as a road, perhaps through the wilderness. Here, I used a teal blue background and soft shades of solid colors for the image, with colored fabric paint outlines. The words were done in lavender outlined with clear glitter fabric paint.

Stir Up Your Power, O Lord, and Come is a traditional Advent prayer. Since there is no central image, the fabric background provides the primary art. It is a beautiful batik cotton with shades of blue and teal and a little light green. The words and corner decorations are royal blue, outlined in matching paint.

Watch, Hope, Prepare, Behold are basic themes of Advent, and this simple banner is an easy one for a beginner. I used a subtle blue batik-style print for the background and a soft solid blue for the candles with yellow flames. The candles and flames are outlined in matching paint.

O Come to Us, Emmanuel was my first Advent banner. I used a silky solid dark turquoise background. The lamp is metallic silver fabric, and ½-inch metallic silver braid is used for the cross and the decoration on the lamp. I used a wider metallic silver braid for borders.

Fling wide

the gates!

The King of Glory

comes!

PREPARE

the WAY of the LORD

Stir up Your power, O Lord, and COME

WATCH

HOPE

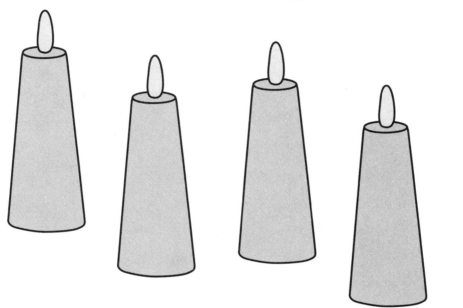

PREPARE

BEHOLD

Christmas and Epiphany

Themes of Christmas and Epiphany are mixed together in popular culture, but are separated in the church calendar because they are different events. Christmas celebrates the birth of Jesus in Bethlehem. Epiphany (which means *manifestation*) celebrates the star that led the Wise Men to the young child Jesus, probably in Nazareth (Luke 2:39). Nativity scenes that include both shepherds and Wise Men combine these two stories, which likely happened a year or more apart. These banners celebrate the arrival of the infant Jesus, the One who would change everything for all time.

Christmas

Ring the Bells! Ring the bells! Let the whole world know! This banner celebrates the birth of Christ and can also be used for the bell choir. It is simple enough to be used as a children's activity, and begs to be done in bright, joyful colors.

Joy to the World and **The Lord Is Come** is a pair of banners using words of a favorite Christmas carol and a traditional design for angels. Angels figure prominently in the Christmas story, so they are appropriate for banners. For this pair I used a solid linen-like deep teal background and a pale, subtle calico print for the angel robes. I outlined each part of the angel design with glued-on gold cord flexible enough to go around all the curves. The lettering is the same calico as the angel robes and is outlined with paint.

She Gave Birth to a Son and **And Laid Him in a Manger** may be used as a pair or individually. If the banner with a manger is used by itself, change the word "And" to "She," using the lettering from the other banner. These designs may be used with the words, or the images can be enlarged and used without words. Pale yellow and off-white calico ovals give the suggestion of a halo and signify the holiness of the Christ Child. A dark blue calico background suggests night. It is virtually impossible to portray human faces in the sort of fabric art used in my banners, so I avoid the attempt and use a more stylized representation of Mary and Jesus.

Epiphany

A Star . . . A Babe . . . Peace with God was my first Epiphany banner. The banner background is a solid dark royal blue, representing the night sky. The star and words are white outlined with clear glitter paint, and the borders are made of wide, shiny white lacey fringe.

Three Crowns and Three Gifts represents the Wise Men and their gifts of gold, frankincense, and myrrh. I did this banner on a background of dark teal calico with a subtle print highlighted with gold. The crowns are metallic gold fabric, and the gifts are light blue with gold accents.

Let the Light Shine and **For All God's Children** is a pair celebrating the light of the Gospel. They introduce the theme of spreading light of Christ throughout the world. The backgrounds are medium blue satin with sparkles on it. The letters are shiny white, outlined with glitter paint. With good lighting, these banners glow!

O Christ the Light, Illuminate our Darkness has a similar theme of the light shining in the darkness. It was done on a deep blue batik print. The words are shiny white satin fabric outlined in clear glitter paint.

Ring

the bells!

JOY to the WORLD

the LORD

is

COME

She gave birth

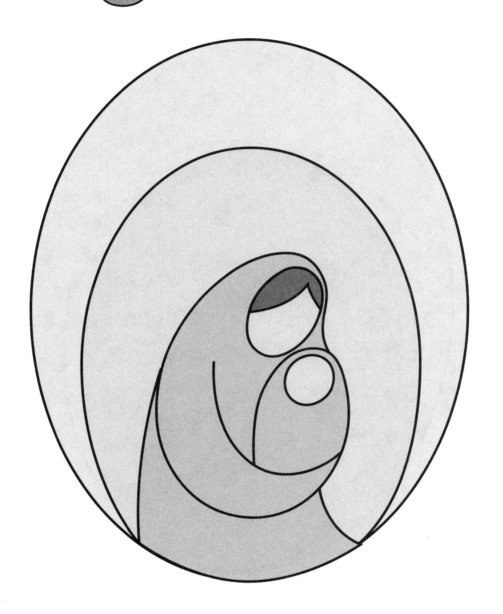

to a Son

...and laid Him

in a manger

A Star...
A Babe...
Peace with God

Let the Light Shine

for All
God's
Children

O Christ The Light, Illuminate Our Darkness

Lent

Lent is a time of reflection, prayer, and renewal. However, my earliest association with the season was hearing my friends at school talk about giving things up for Lent, and as a young adult, I thought I should focus on my own sin and need for repentance. Not surprisingly, Lent was far from my favorite season of the Church Year!

In more recent years I have come to appreciate Lent as a time to refocus on our core Christian beliefs and practices, opening our hearts to God's grace and love. In the process, we are indeed led to let go of some things in order to make more space for the holy One. We come home to God—a homecoming filled with peace and gratitude.

Some of the designs for these Lenten banners could be used at other times as well. The color for Lent is purple.

Lord, Have Mercy and **Hear Our Prayer** are easy to make. Their beauty depends on a combination of striking fabrics. This is another example of using a more dramatic print with a very simple image. I used a gorgeous shades-of-purple cotton print for the crosses and a light rose-purple moiré for the background. The lettering is dark purple and the crosses are outlined in ½-inch purple braid.

Gracious and Merciful and **Abounding in Steadfast Love** are phrases from the Lenten liturgy. The banners were successful experiments using a multicolor floral print, something I rarely do. The backgrounds are solid purple and the diagonal stripes are a floral print of purple, blue, and turquoise, outlined with ¼-inch ribbon that picks up a light turquoise in the print. The words are cut from vinyl upholstery and glued on.

Amazing Grace could be used at any time of year, but I made a banner for Lent using a purple and white satin tie-dye print for the background. The cross and words are shiny white fabric; the cross is outlined with satiny white braid.

I Am the Vine, You Are the Branches are familiar words of Jesus, recorded in John 15. I was inspired to make this banner by a beautiful cotton print with vines and bunches of grapes, which was perfect for a purple background. Since the print is vivid, I used it in a simple swoosh. I used white vinyl upholstery for the lettering, as it holds its shape (important for these elaborate letters), does not need to be outlined, and adds some depth. The curlicues on the letters are reminiscent of grapevines.

The **Baptismal Shell** found on page 78 and the stylized **Chi-Rho** on page 85 are the central designs for another pair of Lenten banners. (A more traditional Chi-Rho pattern in available on page 14.) For these, the background is a print of shades of purple and the images are a light shade of purple outlined with purple braid. Then I added a dark purple frame of 2-inch grosgrain ribbon on all four edges of each banner.

Lord, have

Mercy

Hear our

Prayer

Gracious and Merciful

Abounding in Steadfast Love

Amazing

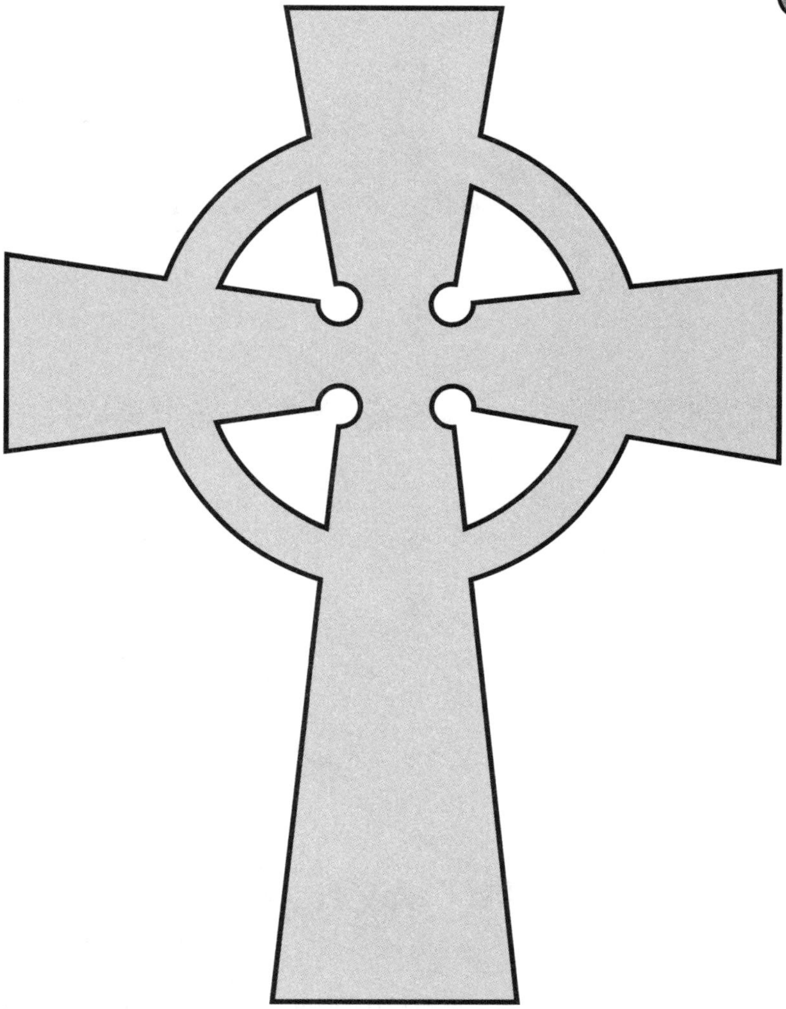

Grace

I am the Vine,

You are the Branches

Holy Week and Using Crosses

Palm Sunday

Palm Sunday begins the most amazing week of the Church Year with powerful events and emotions swirling around and carrying us from the heights of joy to the depths of grief and back. The wild cheers of "Hosanna!" on Palm Sunday give way to the tender sorrow and touching love of Jesus' last supper with His disciples on Maundy Thursday.

Then we join the disciples in the crushing loss of Jesus' death on Good Friday and the numbness and stunned perplexity of Holy Saturday when grief is too fresh and too profound to express. Finally there is the literally incredible news on Easter Sunday—we hear once again that Christ has conquered that ultimate enemy, death, and we are overwhelmed with gratitude and joy.

Hosanna in the Highest, a banner for Palm Sunday, uses white or off-white linen weave background, a green calico with a small or subtle print for the palm branches, and a coordinating green solid or calico for the lettering, outlined with green paint. Carried in procession with children waving palm branches or leaves, it helps us praise the King of kings who entered Jerusalem riding on a donkey, knowing how soon the praise would turn to condemnation.

Maundy Thursday

For Maundy Thursday, consider using the pattern on page 89, **Unto the Least of These**, which portrays foot washing and Jesus' words spoken on that fateful evening. Remove Lenten banners during the stripping of the altar, adding to the sense of solemnity and impending doom.

Good Friday

Worshipers enter the sanctuary in silence for the solemnity of the Good Friday Tenebrae service. Unadorned black paraments are on the altar, the cross may be draped in black, and the pastor wears a black cassock without the usual white alb.

I used eight of the cross designs on pages 39–47 to make a set of black banners for Good Friday. Each banner has a solid black background and a simple cross in a subtle heather tone of blue, lavender, mauve, or tan. There are no borders or words, and the crosses are not outlined. The banners, hung four on each side of the sanctuary, make a quiet but dramatic contribution to the solemnity of the Good Friday service.

The dramatic shifts from the rich purple banners of Lent to the stark black banners of Good Friday to the white and pastel brilliance of Easter banners highlights and enhances the contrasting moods and messages of worship during the deeply significant services of Holy Week and Easter.

Using Crosses for Banners

The cross is the central symbol of Christianity and has been used in countless variations through the centuries. The cross patterns in this section, including the triple cross on page 47, can be used in a variety of ways on banners. Crosses are incorporated into many of the designs in this book (see the index on page 96 for page numbers). You can combine crosses with words of Scripture to make banners for special occasions or emphases.

Choosing various fabrics and colors, as well as adding or omitting decorative outlines or borders, offers unlimited opportunity for creative expression of our deepest beliefs. Pray for the Spirit's guidance and see where you are led.

Easter and Ascension

Easter

Easter is pure joy and celebration! We have walked with Jesus through His passion, death, and burial, and we have walked with the disciples in their stunning loss and grief. On Easter we break forth in festive music and song as we hear again the truly incredible news that Christ has risen from the grave. In northern climates, this occurs in spring, and the hope of the risen Christ blends with the renewal of the earth. The liturgical color is white, although I also use off-white and light shades of blue, green and yellow.

He Is Risen, Joy Abounds uses a subtle calico print with colors of a sunrise and the suggestion of the sun coming up. The calico cross, with its colors of yellow, blue, and subtle peach or orange is framed by a yellow circle, reminiscent of the sun, on a solid off-white background. The cross and circle are outlined with copper-colored paint. The lettering is copper-colored fabric outlined with matching paint, and I used borders of a warm brown braid.

Risen and **Indeed** are taken from the ancient Easter greeting, "Christ is risen" to which we joyfully respond, "He is risen, indeed." This pair is designed to hang where worshipers can easily see both. The originals are hung on a white wall, so I used a light green calico with a subtle design for the background. I used a blue, green, and yellow floral print calico with a white background for the letters and a second, smaller floral print with the same colors for the corner designs. The letters and corner designs were all outlined with hunter green.

Alleluia! is another simple banner that depends on an artistic choice of fabrics for its beauty. Because it is simple, a combination of prints works well as long as you don't introduce too many colors or bold designs. For the background of this banner I used a calico in shades of yellow. The framing stripes are another calico print with turquoise and yellow, outlined with narrow yellow ribbon, and the "Alleluia" is darker turquoise, outlined in matching paint.

Ascension

His the Victory shows the risen Christ departing from earth and returning to heaven. It's hard to imagine how the disciples felt, seeing yet another astounding event. For the banner, the figure of the ascending Christ is light or medium blue on a white cross, and the background is a tie-dye print of blue and white with touches of purple. The words are white, outlined in blue or white. The blue of the background is reminiscent of the sky, although I doubt I would choose a fabric with pictures of clouds on it.

He is Risen

Joy Abounds

Pentecost

On Pentecost, which is observed in late May or early June, we celebrate the coming of the Holy Spirit upon Jesus' apostles as they waited and prayed as He instructed them. The coming of the Holy Spirit was dramatic and resulted in the infant church growing by leaps and bounds.

Pentecost: Power for Witness uses a combination of word art and images. The background is a bright solid red fabric. I was able to find a fabric that has an orange and yellow design that looks something like flames, and the words are yellow calico with a marbleized pattern. The banner is bold and eye-catching and portrays the power that Jesus promised to the disciples when He said, "You will receive power when the Holy Spirit has come upon you, and you will be My witnesses . . . to the end of the earth" (Acts 1:8).

The wordless banners **Dove** and **Wind** were designed to be a pair. The backgrounds are bright red calico with lighter red in a marble pattern. The images are white satin outlined with white paint, and I used wide, heavy white lace for borders. The banners hang behind the altar on an off-white wall. They demonstrate that banners do not need to be elaborate in order to be effective! At my church, the sanctuary is also decorated for Pentecost with banks of bright red geraniums and bunches of helium-filled red balloons. The symbol of a dove for the Holy Spirit comes from Mark 1:10, which says that after Jesus' Baptism, the Spirit descended on Him like a dove. The symbol of wind reminds us that the Holy Spirit first came upon the waiting apostles with "a sound like a mighty rushing wind" (Acts 2:2). It also reminds us that the Spirit is as powerful and unpredictable as wind, blowing and moving wherever it wills (John 3:8).

Fill Us with Love and **Inspire Us to Serve** use the familiar symbols of the dove and flames. The symbol of flames for Pentecost comes from Acts 2:3, where we are told that the Spirit came upon the gathered people like tongues of fire on the day of Pentecost. The themes of the two banners are related. If we are filled with God's love, we will be inspired to serve God and others. The Holy Spirit both fills us with love and inspires us to serve, so these themes are particularly relevant at Pentecost.

These banners are made almost entirely of subtle calico prints: red backgrounds, white-on-white for the dove, brick red for the outer flames and gold for the inner flames, and a tiny brown print for the words. The dove's halo is metallic gold. The dove is outlined with white braid and the flames are outlined with narrow gold braid. The words are outlined with off-white or beige paint.

Cross, Dove, and Globe The wordless images of a haloed dove descending to a globe remind us that the Holy Spirit came for all people and still comes to the whole world. In Genesis 1:2, we are told that the Spirit moved over the creation when it was without form. The Spirit still moves over the face of the earth and all its people, seeking to bring God's plans to fulfillment. The background for this banner is red calico with a subtle design and gold highlights. The dove is white, outlined in gold cord, and the cross is a pale blue, outlined with white cord. The globe is light blue calico with a subtle design, with navy blue cord for the lines and narrow braid around the globe.

pentecost

for power witness

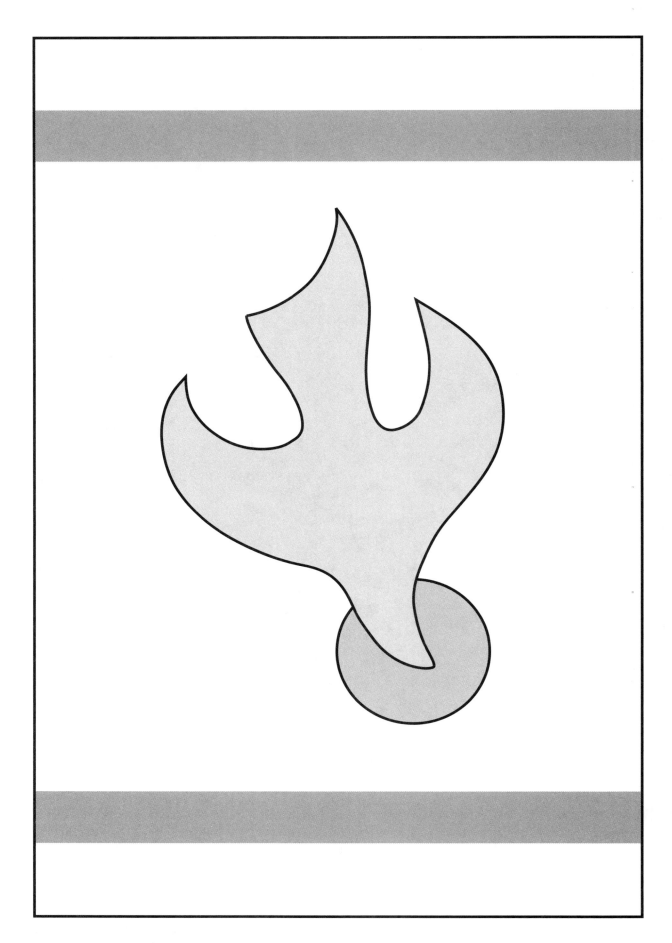

Fill us

with love

Inspire us

to serve

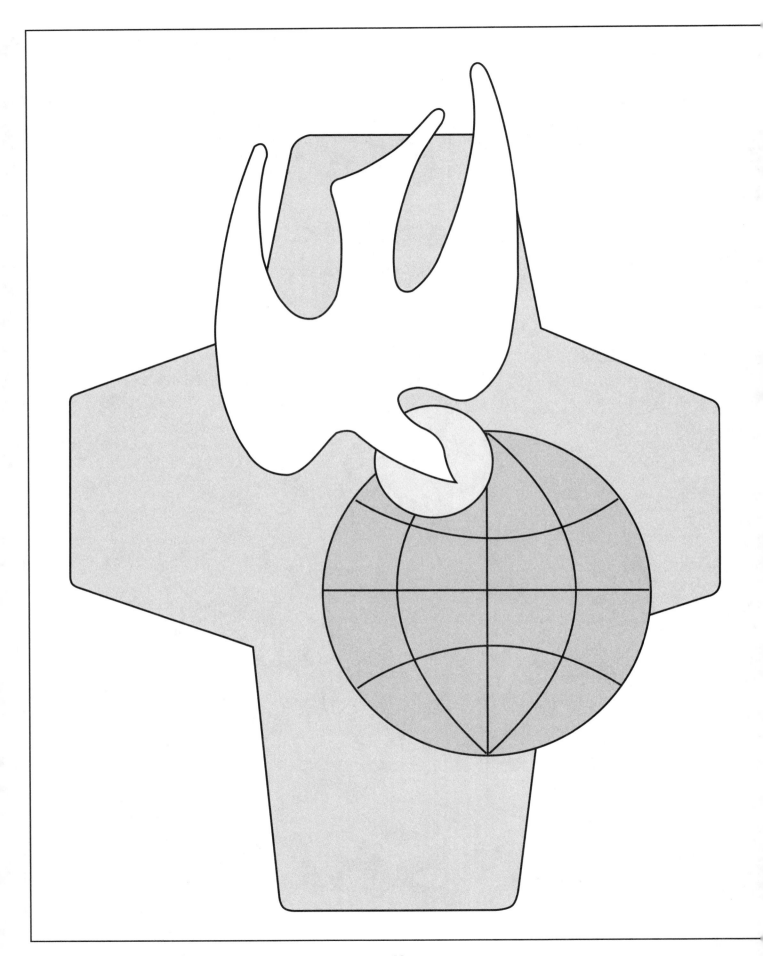

The Close of the Church Year

There are several special commemorations late in the Church Year, just before it ends with Christ the King Sunday.

Reformation

I Will Be Their God and **They Shall Be My People** are words spoken by Jeremiah as he looked forward to a new covenant between God and the people of Israel (Jeremiah 31:33). As Christians, we have taken these ancient words, included in Reformation readings, to define ourselves as well.

For these banners, I used tan upholstery fabric with a rough, coarse weave for the scrolls, dark brown vinyl upholstery for the lettering, and solid red backgrounds. The extra lines on the scrolls were done with dark brown fabric paint, and to suggest rough and uneven edges on the scroll, I used small amounts of brown fabric paint on the edges and smeared it toward the center with my finger.

The **Luther Seal** or **Luther Rose** was designed by Martin Luther himself, and every element of it has symbolic meaning. The original design has a lot of heavy black lines that look great in a woodcut but are difficult to reproduce in a banner. This version was inspired by a stained-glass window.

I used shiny satins in the colors chosen by Luther: a black cross on a red heart; a white rose to which I added a pale gold on the edges of the petals, green leaves, blue background, and a gold ring. I used a light blue solid for the larger background, but you could also use red, as red is the color of the day. The original is actually not a banner, but is a circular cloth below the bowl in our baptismal font.

All Saints

Rejoice in God's Saints commemorates one of my favorite occasions of the Church Year, as we remember and honor those who have gone on before us and also give thanks for the saints who surround us and encourage us in the faith. This banner has a white background; I used a nubbly drapery fabric, but you could also use a white-on-white calico. I used felt for the figures; the hands, feet, and heads of the figures use shades of brown and the robes as well as words are bright colors.

Thanksgiving

Raise Joyful Hearts and **Thanks Be to God** are hung in November, as the Church Year comes to a close. Although Thanksgiving Day is not part of the Church Year, the theme of thanksgiving is prominent in the Bible and in our faith life. These banners have a solid brick red background. The swoosh is an autumn leaf print. It was tricky to find one that had large enough leaves to be visible at a distance without being too gaudy. The words are cut from vinyl upholstery and glued on. The added thickness of the vinyl and its backing make it unnecessary to outline the letters. These banners use the same basic design and letter style as the Lenten banner on page 36. They show that you can use the same basic designs with different words, interpreted with different colors and fabrics, to make a great variety of banners.

Christ the King Sunday

Christ Is King uses traditional symbols for Christ the King Sunday, which is always the last Sunday of the Church Year, immediately preceding Advent. Because these symbols are so familiar, the design can be used with or without the words. This banner can appropriately be a bit flashy, as it celebrates the King of kings and Ruler of the universe.

Colors for Luther Seal

Cross: black

Heart: red

Main parts of petals (1): white

Edges of petals (2): pale gold, pale yellow, or cream

Inner part of large petals (3): gold

Leaves (4): green

Background (5): medium blue

Outer ring (6): gold

Rejoice in God's Saints

Raise Joyful Hearts

Thanks Be to God

Christ

is King

Non-Seasonal Banners

These banners are good for the "long green season" of the Church Year, called the Time of the Church. Since they are not associated with liturgical seasons, other colors may be used.

Love, Joy, Peace is based on the familiar list of fruits of the Spirit in Galatians 5:22. I used a multi-color floral print calico for the words on a solid salmon-colored background with a linen-like texture. The words are outlined in cream-colored paint, and borders of a cream-colored wide lacy braid complete the banner.

Peace, Peace, Peace The background is a solid salmon color and all the designs and letters are calicos. The dove is a white calico with a tiny navy pattern. The large interlocking letters are a navy calico, a small floral print with a bit of salmon, and the other words are coordinating calicos.

In This Place I Will Give Peace The original is a colonial blue calico with a tiny print of white, red, and black. The words and the dove are white-on-white calico. The chalice of metallic gold and dove are placed on a navy blue rectangle with a narrow red ribbon border. I added two quilted borders, a wide one of a deep red calico and a narrower one of black calico. Of course the same design can be used for a banner without the quilting and borders.

Come Join the Dance The figures in the banner invite us to join the dance of life and love enjoyed by the children of God. I used a teal and purple calico print for the background, a subtle lavender calico print behind the figures, and royal blue, purple and deep teal calicos for the robes. The words are a pale blue, and everything is outlined with paint.

God So Loved the World . . . from John 3:16 was designed for an emphasis on global mission. The verse is a well-known statement of our faith. I used a very striking but fairly small calico print of blues and greens with shiny gold highlights for the background, solid royal blue for the cross, and a metallic gold fabric for the globe and words. The cross and globe are outlined with narrow gold braid, and the lines on the globe are done with the same gold braid. The words are not outlined. It is one of my most eye-catching banners.

Well Done, Faithful Servant was designed for a celebration of our church secretary's many years of service, and hangs in the church parlor. The background is pastel blue and the lettering is royal blue. The pitcher is a dusty rose color, the bowl is light brown, and the towel is pale blue. I added some shading with fabric paint applied with a brush. I wrote the honoree's name and years of service in squeeze-bottle paint near the bottom of the banner.

For an unrelated occasion of the retirement of a respected and beloved male colleague, I made a small personal version of this banner with more masculine colors and patterns. He loved it!

And God Said It Is Good! is appropriate for an emphasis on the environment and the earth as God's creation. From top to bottom, I used a print with white clouds on a blue background, a green calico for land, and two shades of blue calico for the sea. All four sections are bonded onto a solid dark royal blue circle, thus creating borders between the sections. The background is off-white and the words are the same royal blue as the circle.

Love

Joy

Peace

In this place I will give PEACE

Come join

the dance

God so loved

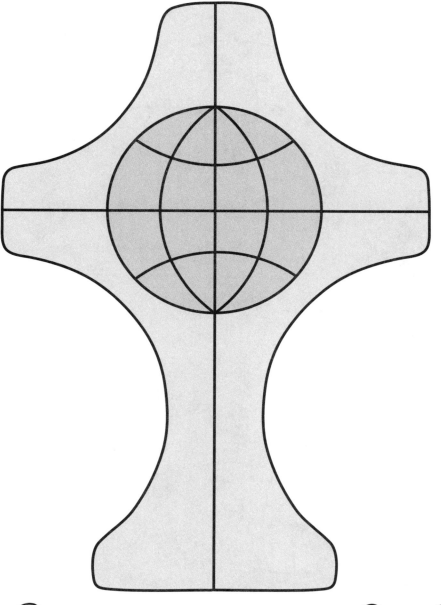

the world...

Well done,

Faithful Servant

and God said

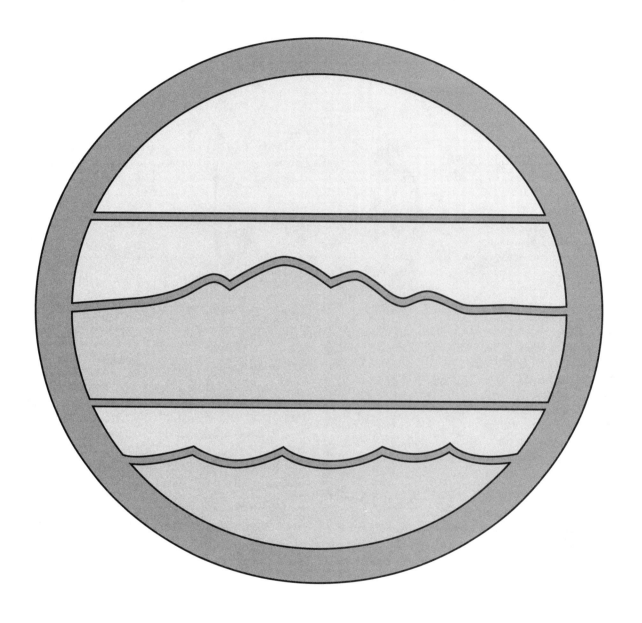

IT IS GOOD!

Christian Symbols

The designs in this section may be used in various colors since they are not associated with any single liturgical season.

Baptism Shell A shell (usually a scallop shell) with three drops of water is an ancient Christian symbol for Baptism in the name of the Father, Son, and Holy Spirit. This design is simple enough for children to make individual Baptism banners with their names on them. Or you may wish to make individual banners to present to newly baptized children or adults as a reminder of their Baptism into Christ. Because the shell is large and simple, it looks best with braid on the lines rather than paint. You can use a somewhat patterned background and a solid color—perhaps a brocade or other textured fabric—for the shell.

Marked with the Cross of Christ As part of the rite of Baptism, we are anointed with water and told, "Receive the sign of the holy cross both upon your forehead and upon your heart to mark you as one redeemed by Christ the crucified." The sign of the cross reminds us that we are redeemed by the Son of God, who suffered and died on a cross on our behalf. In making the sign of the cross, we affirm and proclaim who we are and to whom we belong. This design combines a symbol of Baptism with an all-encompassing cross.

Given for You and **Shed for You** The bread and wine banners are designed to be a pair, so the colors and styles used for the backgrounds, images, and words should coordinate.

Use light brown for the bread and a coordinating pale golden brown for the wheat. The bread on this banner, as well as the wheat from which it is made, represents the body of Christ given to us in Holy Communion. Wheat is also a symbol of prosperity and fruitfulness. Since the bread and wheat are light brown or gold, it is good to use a colorful background with a coordinating fabric for the lettering. Avoid strong patterns, as they would detract from the central design.

Use purple for the grapes, green for the grapevine and leaves, and gold for the chalice. The chalice on this banner symbolizes Holy Communion and the blood shed by Jesus on the cross for forgiveness of our sins. Grapes are the source of the wine, and also symbolize the fruitfulness of the Christian life.

Holy Trinity The triangle, with its three sides and three points, represents the Trinity, as does the trefoil, formed from three partially overlapping circles. These two symbols are often combined; this version uses a bit of artistic variation on the basic design. I used a marbleized print of green with gold highlights for the background and two shades of gold satin for the triangle and trefoil, outlined with narrow gold braid.

Alpha and Omega The first and last letters of the Greek alphabet symbolize that God is the beginning and the end of all things (Revelation 1:8). I used the trinity symbol from **Holy Trinity** (above) without words and the Alpha and Omega to make a pair, using the color scheme described above.

Thy Word Is a Lamp The burning lamp is traditionally associated with worship and symbolizes God's presence among us. The lamp also stands for wisdom and knowledge, and reminds us that God's Word is our guide and our light, showing us where to go. Choose colors and fabrics according to how and where the banner will be used.

Chi-Rho See pages 14, 18, 44, and 85. The Chi-Rho is one of the earliest Christian symbols. It consists of the first two letters of the Greek word for Christ, the Anointed (XP) superimposed on one another. Thus it represents Christ, the Messiah. This symbol can be interpreted artistically in many ways, so let creativity be your guide.

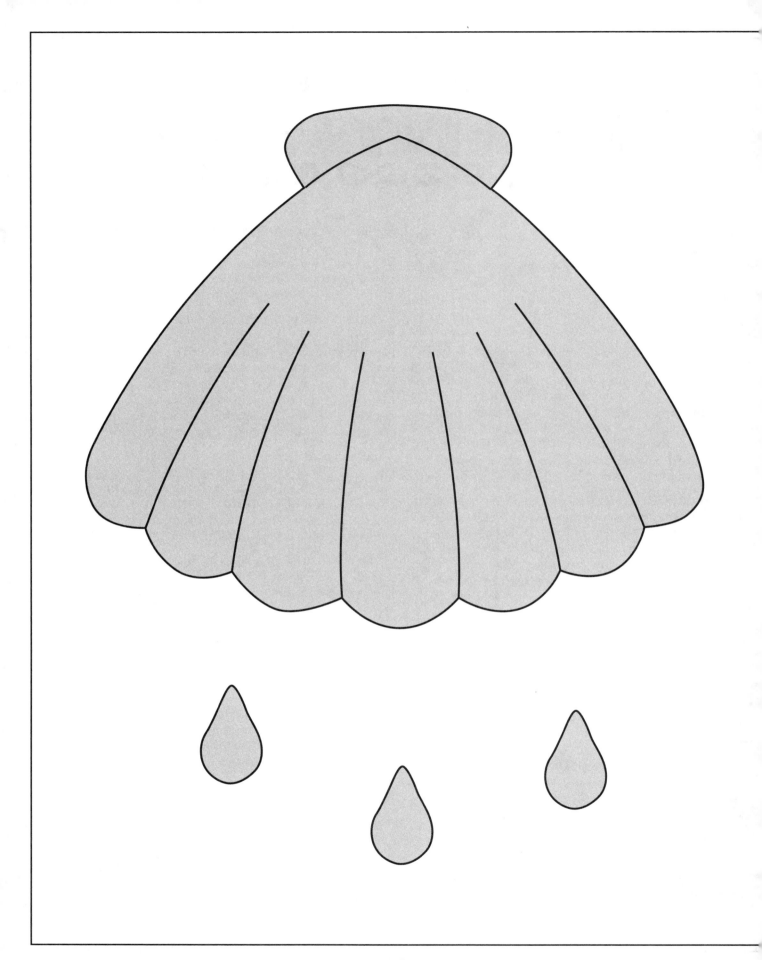

Marked with the

Cross of Christ

given for you

shed for you

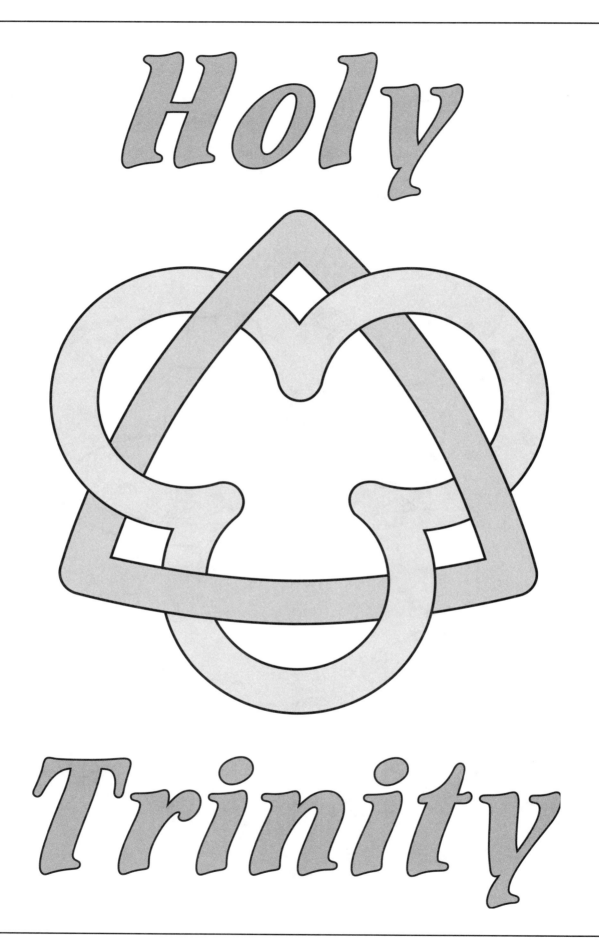

Thy Word

is a Lamp

Church Boards

This set of banners was also designed for use during the Time of the Church, the "long green season" between Pentecost (which occurs in late May or early June) and Advent, unmarked by special festivals. The Time of the Church is a chance to recognize the various boards of the congregation and their service to the local church. Church board banners celebrate the "behind the scenes" committee work done by lay members of the congregation. The banners in this section have backgrounds of shades of blue, turquoise, teal and green—cool colors that blend well with the liturgical color of the season. Names of boards are written in script using fabric paint, just above the lower border. Designs and words are outlined with matching fabric paint.

These banners can also be used in other settings, such as hanging a Christian education banner near Sunday School rooms or a worship and music banner in the choir room. The church where I'm a member used this set to decorate the fellowship hall for a "job fair" effort to recruit new board members.

All of these banners have borders (see next section). The originals are 36 inches wide and 54 to 60 inches long, using the designs and words on pages 87–94. You can adapt the designs for different sizes or shapes of banners.

I had a lot of fun and used a lot of colors in crafting these banners. Looking for materials to use for borders was a treasure hunt; finding solid colors for the central images that coordinated with the borders was a creative challenge. I did not use much calico in making this set, partly because the images have more detail and might look a bit cluttered if done in prints. I hope you enjoy making these banners as much as I did!

Borders

All of the church board banners have solid color backgrounds and bold borders that are integral to the overall design. There are many possibilities for banner borders besides long silky fringe. Besides what is shown here, options include wide lace, wide ribbon and plainer fabrics.

Worship and Music—page 87. A cotton calico print border adds interest and reinforces the theme. The outline is fabric paint.

Christian Education—page 88. A winsome design and hearts on a quilt print carry out the theme and mood as well as color. The outline is fabric paint.

Social Ministry—page 89. For this border, a shiny taffeta home decorator fabric is layered on top of a solid fabric. The outline is fabric paint.

Outreach and Welcome—page 90. A block design of a cotton print and the color combination make it a good choice for a border. The outline is fabric paint.

Stewardship—page 91. This border is a striped print of black, white, and teal with black braid added to the edges to give it more definition.

Finance—page 92. A bold cotton fringe in a deeper shade of the background color is a good choice. Home decoration departments carry a variety of heavy fringes.

Property—page 93. A colorful cotton braid, about 2 inches wide, is a good border. The colors of the design should be chosen to match.

Mutual Ministry—page 94. Bold, clear colors in cotton blend will be picked up in the robes of the figures. The outline is fabric paint.

Sing to the Lord

Let the little

children come

...unto the

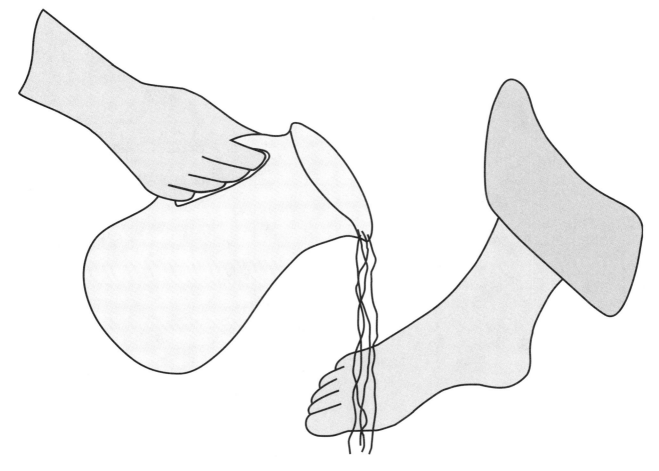

least

of these

GATHER US IN

We give Thee

but

Thine own

FAITHFUL STEWARDS

OF GOD'S GIFTS

BLESS THE WORK OF OUR HANDS

HONOR THOSE WHO LEAD

Index of Word Sources

Index of Themes and Images

A
Advent 12–18
All Saints 65
Alpha and omega 83
Angels 21–22
Ascension 53

B
Baby Jesus 23–24
Baptism 78–79
Bells 20
Bible/Word 84, 88
Bread 80

C
Candles 17
Celtic crosses 35
Chalice 72, 81
Chi-Rho 14, 18, 44, 85
Children 88
Christ the king 68
Christian education 88
Christmas 19–24
Church 90
Church boards 86–94
Communion 72, 80–81
Creation 76
Cross 14, 18, 31–32, 35, 39–47,
    49 ,53, 55, 60, 64, 68, 74,
    79, 85–85, 94
Crowns 26, 53, 68

D
Dance 73
Dove 56, 58–59, 60, 71–72

E
Earth 74, 76, 60
Easter 48–52
Epiphany 25–29
Eucharist 72, 80–81

F
Finance 92
Fire 55, 58–59

G
Gates 13
Gifts 26
Giving 91
Globe 60, 74
Good Friday 39–47
Grace 35
Grapes 81

H
Hands 91, 93

J
Joy 21, 49, 66, 70

K
King 14, 68

L
Lamp 18, 84
Leaders 94
Lent 14, 30–36, 78, 85
Light 18, 27–29, 84
Love 33–34, 58–59, 70, 74, 88
Luther rose/seal 64

M
Manger 24
Mary and baby Jesus 23
Maundy Thursday 89
Mercy 31, 33
Music 87

O
Outreach 90

P
Palm Sunday 38
Peace 25, 71–72
Pentecost 54–60
Prayer 31–32
Property 93

R
Reformation 62–64

S
Saints 65
Scale 92
Scroll 62–63
Service 58–60, 75
Shell 78
Sing 87
Social ministry 89
Star 25, 26
Stewardship 91–93

T
Thanksgiving 66–67
Trinity 82

V
Vine 36

W
Wash feet 89
Wheat 80
Wind 57
Wine 72, 81
Witness 55